50 STATES TO CELEBRATE

Celebrating
GEORGIA

The text of this book is set in Weidemann.
The display type is set in Bernard Gothic.
The illustrations are drawn with pencil and colored digitally.
The maps are pen, ink, and watercolor.

Photograph of right whale and calf on page 32 © 2015 by NOAA/NMFS as "Right whale and calf" under Creative Commons license 2.0
Photograph of bobwhite on page 32 © 2015 by Jeffers/Fotolia
Photograph of Cherokee rose on page 32 © 2015 by Georgia Department of Economic Development

Library of Congress Cataloging-in-Publication Data
Kurtz, Jane.
Celebrating Georgia / Jane Kurtz ; illustrated by C. B. Canga.
p. cm. — (Green light readers level 3)
ISBN 978-0-544-41975-9 paperback
ISBN 978-0-544-41976-6 paper over board
1. Georgia—Geography—Juvenile literature. I. Canga, C. B. II. Title.
F286.3.K87 2014
975.8—dc23
2014023534

Manufactured in China
SCP 10 9 8 7 6 5 4 3 2 1
4500521812

50 STATES TO CELEBRATE

Celebrating
GEORGIA

Written by **Jane Kurtz**
Illustrated by **C. B. Canga**

Green Light Readers
Houghton Mifflin Harcourt
Boston   New York

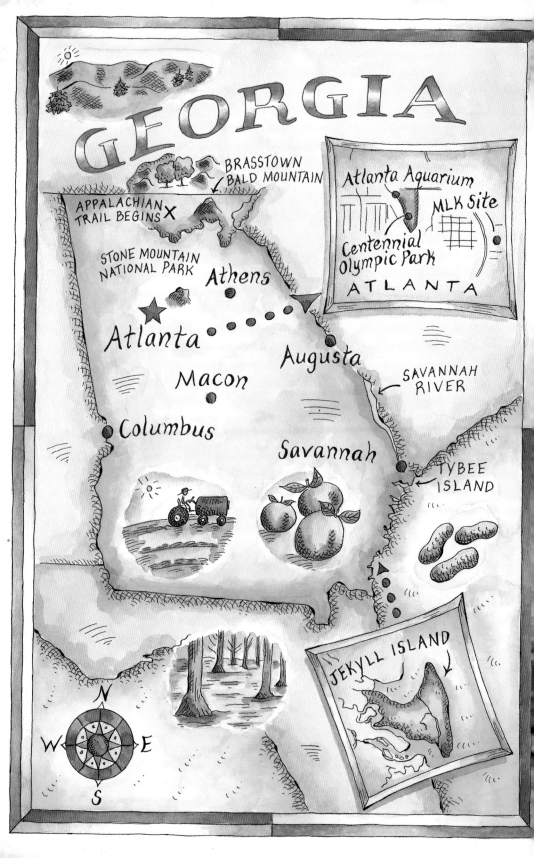

Hi, I'm Mr. Geo.
Can you guess where I am?
I'm biting into a sweet, juicy peach.
In fact, I'm in the Peach State.
That's right! I'm in Georgia.

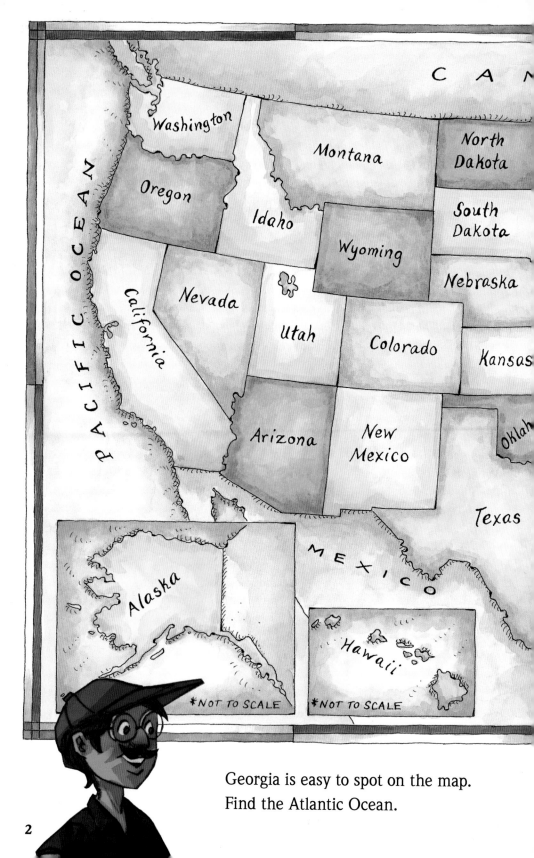

Georgia is easy to spot on the map.
Find the Atlantic Ocean.

2

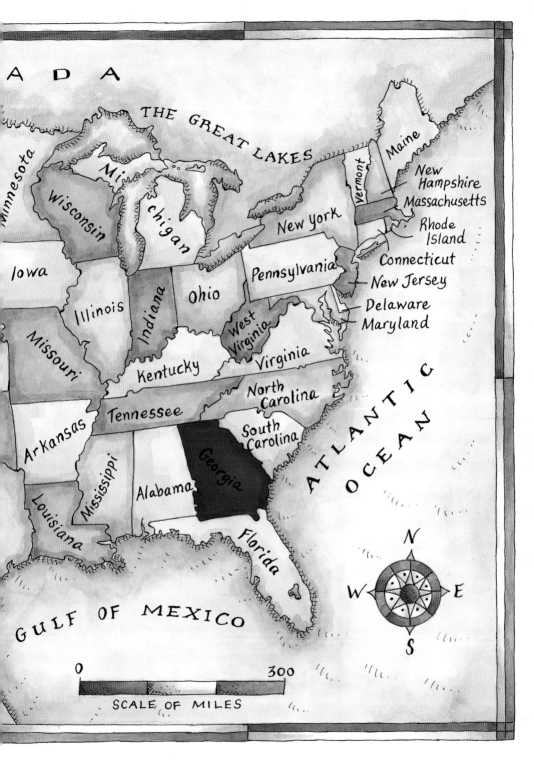

Look north of Florida.
Now look east of Alabama.
You can't miss Georgia!

My first stop is the Georgia Peach Festival.
I'm helping to stir the world's biggest peach **cobbler**.
Shall we use this boat paddle for our tasting spoon?
Open wide for a sweet treat!

Did you know?

Peaches are an important Georgia crop.
Farmers grow about 86 million pounds of
them a year.

Now that my taste buds are all warmed up,
I plan to sample a big slice of pecan pie.
In the fall, I can shake fresh pecans from a tree.

I planned to shake a peanut tree, too.

Oops! Peanuts grow underground.

About half of America's peanuts grow in Georgia.

Did you know?

Jimmy Carter, the 39th president of the United States, was once a peanut farmer in Plains, Georgia.

Georgia's first people were Native Americans.
They grew corn, beans, and pumpkins.
They built homes with a mixture of
sticks, grass, mud, and **reeds**.
Some created amazing mound structures . . .

. . . and played a game called **chunkey**.

It's a little like stickball.

I hope I catch on fast!

Did you know?

The Creek people and the Cherokee lived in Georgia long before the English came and established it as the 13th **colony.**

Did you know?

Juliette Gordon Low, the founder of the Girl Scouts, is from Savannah. Her family home is open for tours.

The first English settlers came to Georgia in 1733.
They carefully planned the city of Savannah,
high on a **bluff,** on a river and near the sea.
It's full of pretty parks and charming squares,
and the shadiest oak trees I've ever seen!

Ready to head to the islands near Savannah?

We'll find beaches, lighthouses, and cooling breezes.

Pirates used to hide their treasure on Tybee Island.

For me, the treasure is here on Jekyll Island:

baby turtles making their way to the sea!

I can see wondrous creatures
at the Great Okefenokee **Swamp**, too.
I spotted an otter slipping and sliding on a rock.
I'm glad that alligator didn't spot me!

Did you know?

The fly catcher and sundew are two plants
in the Okefenokee Swamp that eat bugs.

Georgia was once home to
many cotton **plantations.**
Visiting old mansions, barns, cabins, and forts
gives me a peek at daily life
before the **Civil War.**

Enslaved Africans worked long hours,
planting and picking cotton in fields.
They did many hard jobs.
They had no freedom until
the Civil War helped end slavery
in our country in 1865.

The Georgia Civil War Heritage Trails highlight
places where soldiers from the Northern and
Southern states battled each other.

Here I am in Atlanta, the capital of Georgia.
Welcome to the coolest place in town,
the Fountain of Rings at Centennial Olympic Park.
Sometimes the five rings spray.
Sometimes the five rings splash.
Sometimes they put on a dazzling light show . . .

But no matter what, they always remind me that this city hosted the Olympic Games in 1996.

Did you know?

The water in the Fountain of Rings is recycled to irrigate the trees in the park.

One of America's most admired
leaders and dreamers was born in Atlanta.
His name was Martin Luther King Jr.
We can see where he lived as a child and
hear his voice in the church where he preached.
He spoke out bravely about equal rights for all.

Today I walked in the actual footsteps of **civil rights** heroes.

The footprints of the activist Rosa Parks, the poet Maya Angelou, and the baseball player Hank Aaron are preserved at the Intl. Civil Rights Walk of Fame.

Atlanta is a big, busy city.

Some major companies got their start here.

At CNN headquarters, we can learn about the news business.

Do I look natural in front of the camera?

A very popular drink was invented in Atlanta.
I'm seated at an old-fashioned soda fountain
where it was first served.
It's here at the World of Coca-Cola.
So is the **vault** that holds the secret recipe.
I wish I knew the combination.

A pharmacist named John Pemberton
invented Coca-Cola in 1886.

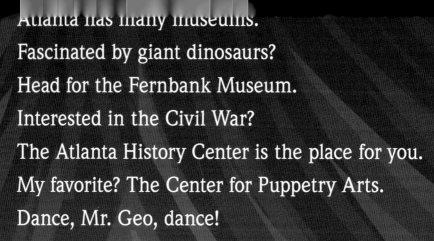

Atlanta has many museums.

Fascinated by giant dinosaurs?

Head for the Fernbank Museum.

Interested in the Civil War?

The Atlanta History Center is the place for you.

My favorite? The Center for Puppetry Arts.

Dance, Mr. Geo, dance!

Sports fans have fun in Atlanta too.
I don't swing hard enough to play for the Braves.
I don't dribble fast enough to play for the Hawks.
I'm not brawny enough to play for the Falcons.
But I have enough energy to run
the Peachtree Road Race!

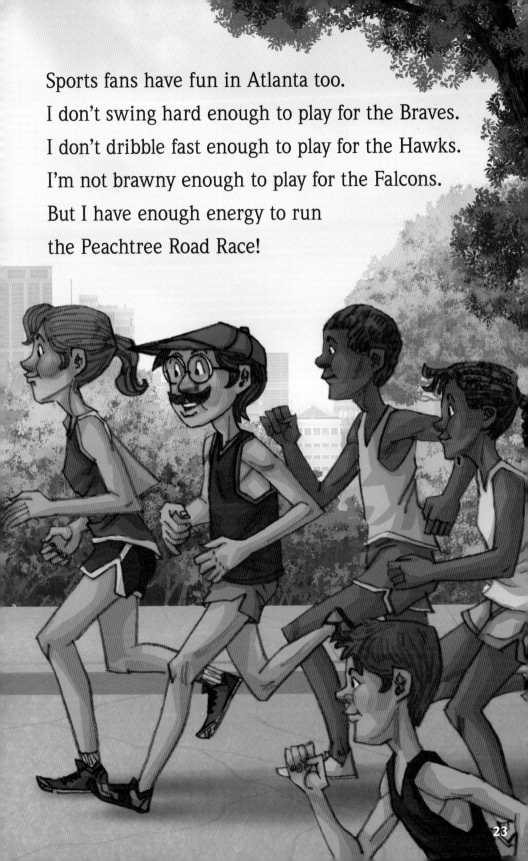

Are you an animal fan?

These cute pandas are visitors to Georgia.

Just like me.

But this kingsnake lives in Atlanta backyards.

I get to see it up close at Zoo Atlanta.

Just not *too* close!

 **Did you know?**

Georgia is home to about 55 **species** of snakes.

Here at the Georgia Aquarium, I touched a stingray and other sea animals that live in tide pools.
What amazed me most?
Watching the beautiful beluga whales!

Right whales are Georgia's state marine mammal. Many give birth to their calves in the state's coastal waters.

Near Atlanta, I enjoy Stone Mountain National Park. I can ride a cable car to the top of the mountain and zoom all the way down!

The carvings on Stone Mountain are of Southern leaders from the Civil War—Jefferson Davis, Robert E. Lee, and Stonewall Jackson.

I love exploring in Georgia's Blue Ridge
Mountains, too.

The famous **Appalachian Trail** begins there.

Today, I hiked to Amicalola Falls.

It sure is tall and tumbling!

Did you know? The Appalachian Trail is about 2,200 miles
long and goes through 14 states.

Next stop?

Dahlonega on the Chestatee River.

A gold rush started here in 1828.

I just toured an old underground mine.

Now I'm learning how to pan for gold.

Wish me luck!

My journey ends atop Brasstown Bald Mountain.
It's the highest spot in Georgia.
I can look down for half a mile to the beautiful
valleys below.

I see places I visited.

I see new adventures waiting.

Georgia will be on my mind for a long time.

Fast Facts About Georgia

Nickname: The Peach State

State motto: Wisdom, Justice, and Moderation

State capital: Atlanta

Other major cities: Columbus, Augusta, Savannah, Athens, Roswell, Macon

State mammal: Right whale

State bird: Bobwhite

State flower: Cherokee rose

State flag:

Population: Approximately 9.9 million according to 2013 U.S. Census.

Fun facts: This state has around 55 streets with the name Peachtree. Marble from Georgia was used to create the statue of Abraham Lincoln at the Lincoln Memorial in Washington, D.C.

Dates in Georgia History

800–1600: Ancestors of the Cherokee people and the Creek build mound structures.

1733: James Oglethorpe establishes the first English settlement in Savannah.

1793: Eli Whitney invents the cotton gin in Georgia.

1828–29: The Georgia gold rush begins.

1838: The U.S. government forces the Cherokee to leave their homeland in Georgia and march west to what is now Oklahoma.

1861: Georgia **secedes** from the Unites States and joins the **Confederate States of America** during the Civil War.

1864: Atlanta is burned down during the Civil War.

1865: The Civil War ends.

1870: Georgia is readmitted to the United States.

1929: Martin Luther King, Jr., is born in Atlanta.

1968: The Appalachian Trail is named as one of the two first national scenic trails. The first section of the trail opened in 1923; the final section was completed in 1937.

1977: Jimmy Carter, a Georgia governor and peanut farmer, becomes the 39th president of the United States.

1995: The Atlanta Braves win the World Series.

1996: Atlanta hosts the Summer Olympic Games.

Activities

1. **LOCATE** the five states that border Georgia. Which states are to the north? Which state is to the south? Which state is to the east? Which state is west? **SAY** the name of each state out loud.

2. **DESIGN** a magazine page about fun things to see and do in Georgia. Include words and pictures on your magazine page.

3. **SHARE** two facts you learned about Georgia with a family member or friend.

4. **PRETEND** you are the governor of Georgia and a TV travel reporter is going to interview you for a travel show on great places to visit. Other governors will be interviewed too. You want to be the best, so you do some extra research. If you can answer the following questions correctly, you will be a big hit!

    a. **WHO** is the U.S. president who was once the governor of Georgia and also a peanut farmer?

    b. **WHEN** did the first English settlers come to Georgia?

    c. **WHERE** in Georgia did pirates once hide treasure?

    d. In **WHAT** city was Martin Luther King Jr. born?

5. **UNJUMBLE** these words that have something to do with Georgia. Write your answers on a separate sheet of paper.

    a. **STANEPU** (HINT: they grow underground)

    b. **NLTAAAT** (HINT: the state capital)

    c. **VHASNANA** (HINT: another Georgia city)

    d. **HPAEC** (HINT: a Georgia fruit)

    FOR ANSWERS, SEE PAGE 36.

Glossary

Appalachian Trail: a marked hiking trail in the eastern United States extending between Springer Mountain in Georgia and Mount Katahdin in Maine; it runs approximately 2,200 miles through 14 states. (p. 28)

bluff: a steep cliff. (p. 11)

chunkey: a Native American game played by rolling disk-shaped stones across the ground and throwing poles at them in an attempt to place the pole as close to the stopped stone as possible. (p. 9)

civil rights: The rights belonging to all citizens, including freedom from discrimination. (p. 19)

Civil War: the war between the Northern states and the Southern states that helped end slavery in our country. (p. 14)

cobbler: a fruit pie topped with a biscuit crust and baked in a deep dish. (p. 4)

colony: a settlement ruled by another country. (p. 9)

Confederate States of America: the group of 11 Southern states that separated from the United States from 1861–65 and fought in the Civil War against the United States. (p. 33)

plantation: a large farm where crops are grown. (p. 14)

reed: a kind of tall grass with a hollow stem that grows in wet places. (p. 8)

species: a group of plants, animals, or other organisms that are very similar to each other. (p. 24)

swamp: a soft, wet area of land. (p. 13)

vault: a room or compartment where valuable items are placed for safekeeping. (p. 21)

Answers to Activities on page 34:

1) North Carolina and Tennessee are to the North; Florida is to the South; South Carolina is to the east; and Alabama is west; 2) Drawings will vary; 3) Answers will vary; 4a) Jimmy Carter, 4b) 1733, 4c) Tybee Island, 4d) Atlanta; 5a) peanuts, 5b) Atlanta, 5c) Savannah, 5d) Peach.